Children of the World

For a free color catalog describing Gareth Stevens' list of high-quality children's books, call 1-800-341-3569 (USA) or 1-800-461-9120 (Canada).

For their help in the preparation of *Children of the World: USSR*, the editors gratefully thank Helen Prokudina, Information Department of the Soviet Embassy, Washington, DC, and Dr. Z. Geller, Milwaukee, Wisconsin.

Library of Congress Cataloging-in-Publication Data

USSR.

    (Children of the world)
    Includes index.
    Summary: Presents the life of a young child in the Soviet Union, describing the family life, home, school, food, religion, customs, amusements, traditions and celebrations of the country.
    1. Soviet Union—Juvenile literature. [1. Family life—Soviet Union. 2. Soviet Union—Social life and customs] I. Brown, Julie, 1962-   . II. Miyajima, Yasuhiko, 1951-   ill.
DK17.U237   1989   947   88-42891
ISBN 1-55532-215-8

North American edition first published in 1989 by

Gareth Stevens Children's Books
RiverCenter Building, Suite 201
1555 North RiverCenter Drive
Milwaukee, Wisconsin 53212, USA

Series editor: Rhoda Irene Sherwood
Research editor: Scott Enk
Map design: Sheri Gibbs

Printed in the United States of America

1 2 3 4 5 6 7 8 9 95 94 93 92 91 90

Children of the World
USSR

Photographs by
Yasuhiko Miyajima

Edited by
Julie Brown,
Robert Brown,
Susan Taylor-Boyd,
and Rita Reitci

Gareth Stevens Children's Books
MILWAUKEE

. . . a note about *Children of the World*:

The children of the world live in fishing towns, Arctic regions, and urban centers, on islands and in mountain valleys, on sheep ranches and fruit farms. This series follows one child in each country through the pattern of his or her life. Candid photographs show the children with their families, at school, at play, and in their communities. The text describes the dreams of the children and, often through their own words, tells how they see themselves and their lives.

Each book also explores events that are unique to the country in which the child lives, including festivals, religious ceremonies, and national holidays. The *Children of the World* series does more than tell about foreign countries. It introduces the children of each country and shows readers what it is like to be a child in that country.

. . . and about *USSR*:

Ekaterina Aleksandr, whose nickname is Katya, lives in Moscow, the capital of the Soviet Union. Her father is a welder in an auto garage, and her mother is a school nurse. Katya attends a public school, is in the fourth grade, and eagerly awaits the warmer weather in Moscow so she can have more family outings.

To enhance this book's value in libraries and classrooms, comprehensive reference sections include up-to-date information about the Soviet Union's geography, demographics, culture, language, currency, education, industry, and natural resources. *USSR* also features a bibliography, research topics, activity projects, and discussions of such subjects as Moscow, the country's history, political system, and ethnic and religious composition.

The living conditions and experiences of children in the Soviet Union vary tremendously according to economic, environmental, and ethnic circumstances. The reference sections help bring to life for young readers the diversity and richness of the culture and heritage of the Soviet Union. Of particular interest are discussions of the Russian Revolution, the role of the Soviet Union in world politics, and the variety of landscapes and cultures within the vast geographic boundaries of the Soviet Union.

CONTENTS

Katya's family bundles up against the cold. From left: Her mother, Olya, Katya, and her father, Sasha.

LIVING IN THE USSR:
Katya, an Apartment Dweller in Moscow

Katya is a ten-year-old girl living in Moscow, the capital of the Union of Soviet Socialist Republics (USSR). Katya's nation, also known as the Soviet Union, takes up over one-seventh of the world's land and has the largest territory of any nation in the world.

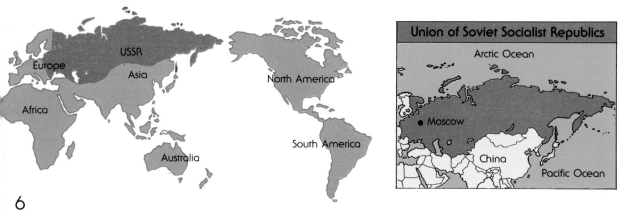

Katya's full name is Ekaterina Aleksandr, but few Russians go by these long, formal names. So she uses a nickname, Katya. Her father is Aleksandr, but he goes by Sasha, and even her mother, with the short name Olga, has a nickname, Olya.

The apartment where Katya lives with her parents is on Kutuzovsky Avenue, a main thoroughfare in Moscow. The building has 110 units, each one about 400 square feet (37 sq m). Every apartment has two rooms, plus a bathroom and a kitchen. Because the ceilings are over 14 feet (4.4 m) high, the apartments don't seem cramped.

Katya must use a complicated way of entering her building. Behind the front door stands another door that is securely locked. On the wall nearby is a panel of numbered buttons. Katya has to push a certain sequence of numbers to unlock the door. Everyone in the building knows the code. This protection against burglary is common throughout the USSR.

Katya's 12-story apartment building.

Residents take pride in keeping their common hallways clean.

Moscow winters are cold. If the temperature drops below -4°F (-20°C), children have to stay indoors because of the danger of frostbite.

Winter in Moscow

Winters in Moscow are harsh. The temperatures can drop to -4°F (-20°C), and strong winds often blow. But the people often joke about the temperature. And they don't let the weather interfere with their activities. Moscow's streets are almost always busy with people.

Katya bundles up against the cold. She knows that any part of her face exposed to the cold turns bright red. Too much exposure can lead to frostbite, so many people in Moscow wear fur hats and coats. They wrap their collars up around their cheeks or use a scarf. And everyone wears mittens or gloves. But when they get indoors, they often wear short sleeves. Their dwellings are always warm, no matter how cold it is outside!

People crowd around a street vendor selling barbecued lamb, called shashlyk.

Low temperatures don't stop the Muscovites.

When Katya waits for a trolley in the winter cold, she is sometimes horribly uncomfortable.

To keep away the cold as they wait for transportation, people can eat something hot. Street vendors sell different kinds of hot foods. Katya often buys *shashlyk*, or barbecued lamb, and *pirozhki*, or dumplings stuffed with beef. The wait isn't long, since the trolleys come often.

Katya walks to school, a risky job on frozen sidewalks.

Katya's school — Number 711.

Katya's School

Katya's school opened in 1954. It is called Moscow Kiev District School Number 711. In the Soviet Union, all schools except universities and colleges have numbers instead of names. School Number 711 has 760 students in grades one through ten. There are 21 classes and 45 teachers. Katya is now in the fourth grade. There are two fourth-grade classes at the school, Class A and Class B, and Katya is in Class A. There are 31 students in Katya's class.

Class A, Katya's fourth-grade class. Two students were absent when this picture was taken.

In Moscow there are about 1,200 academic schools that combine the primary and secondary grades. Students start school when they are seven years old and usually attend through at least the eighth grade. After eighth grade some students choose to transfer to an occupational training program. The ones who stay in the academic school plan to go on to a university. The students in Katya's class all plan to stay past the eighth grade.

Katya works out a problem.

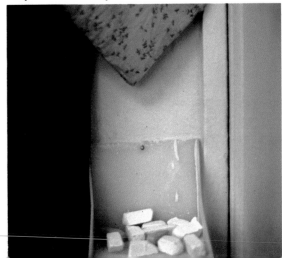

In the Classroom

Classrooms in the Soviet Union are very quiet and orderly. The children sit at desks that are arranged in rows and all facing forward. The teacher talks to the students from the front of the room. Today she calls on Katya to do a math problem at the board. As Katya works out the problem, she shows all the steps to the solution. When she drops her chalk, a few of the children giggle. It's hard to be quiet all the time!

Sometimes Katya must recite passages from literature. When answering in class, she stands next to her desk. Everyone in Katya's class wears a school uniform, but adds a colorful sweater or vivid socks for a cheerful accent. And you can't miss their bright red kerchiefs. These kerchiefs are the Young Pioneer scarves, and they take their color from the Soviet flag.

Chalk is never wasted.

Every classroom has a portrait of Vladimir I.
Lenin, the first leader of the Soviet Union.

The Young Pioneers are a youth organization that is sponsored by the Communist party. Katya folds her kerchief into a triangle and ties it on with a special knot. Her parents used to wear these kerchiefs when they went to school.

Katya's favorite class is literature. Many Russian writers are well known outside of the Soviet Union. Leo Tolstoy, Anton Chekhov, and Maxim Gorky are a few of the writers that are known and read throughout the world in many different languages.

Today Katya's class is studying the poems of Aleksandr Pushkin, the national poet of the Soviet Union. Katya has memorized three of Pushkin's poems already. The students and their teacher, Korojna Origa, take turns reading his poetry out loud.

Everyone pays close attention.

An important part of their education is learning about culture. Katya's class frequently attends special performances for children of the ballets, concerts, plays, and other presentations that are a rich part of Moscow life. To help them follow a performance more easily, the students will learn something about it ahead of time.

Class discussion can get very intense.

Most Soviet citizens enjoy the cultural activities, which the government sponsors. Tickets aren't expensive, but they are difficult to get because the presentations are so popular. The Bolshoi Ballet, well known all over the world, dances in Moscow. There are also many museums and theaters, as well as the famous Moscow Circus.

The schedule of classes is posted on the wall outside the classroom.

Katya especially likes learning about the folk dances and the other arts of all the different nationalities that make up her vast country. The Soviet Union encourages ethnic groups to maintain their culture.

Recesses can last from 10 to 20 minutes.

Katya and her friends rush outside to play.

Time for Recess

If Katya ever fell behind in her studies, she could go for extra help after school. Here she could catch up on work or try to clear up the parts of a course she might not understand. The competition to get into a university is fierce, so students must be near the top of their class. They earn grades on a scale of one to five, with five as the highest possible grade. Most students want to get fours and fives, so they ask for extra coaching after school to raise their grades.

But students don't work all the time. Twice a day they get recesses for meals. There is plenty of talking and laughing as friends eat together and later wait in hallways for their classes to resume. Often Katya and her friends hurry through their meals so they can quickly dress in their outer garments and rush outside. There they can play in the snow. Sometimes they will bring their ice skates to school and spend recess time skating on the playground that is frozen into a skating rink.

The children also tow toboggans to school so they can go tobogganing during recess and after school. The students learn how to ice-skate and ski in physical education class. Katya's class carries their skis to a nearby hill for an hour of instruction and fun. Many times the children stay on after school to get in more skiing and ice skating.

On a winter's day, a hot lunch is welcomed.

Cafeteria lunches are cheap, hot, and tasty.

At Katya's school the morning recess comes after second period. This recess is twenty minutes long and many of the students rush to the cafeteria to buy some breakfast.

The government of the USSR encourages both parents to work, but that often means that no one has time in the morning to prepare breakfast. So Soviet schools take over that responsibility. Maria, Katya's friend, says, "Mornings are a battle to get everyone off on time, so we can't make anything nutritious. School gives us food that's good for us."

Breakfast in the Soviet Union usually consists of cheese, black tea, and the dark brown bread that is served with every meal. Lunch consists of soup such as *borscht* and chicken dishes. Dinners include meats, fish, and vegetables.

Anyone can buy fruit and bread in the cafeteria.

A group of teachers eating lunch.

The principal at Katya's school.

Most teachers are women. They are devoted to the welfare of the children in their charge. Although the teaching profession is highly respected, the pay is low.

Maria Pronina is the principal of Katya's school. She is mainly concerned about, first, peace, and second, good health for everyone.

17

After-school Activities

Schools do not sponsor club activities. Instead, the students go to activities outside of school. Katya attends a class in Finlandic folk dancing. Katya loves this class. "It's romantic," she says. "It's like entering the world of fairy tales." The dances tell a story for Katya.

Some of Katya's friends are learning how to play musical instruments. Others are taking classes in chess, a game that is very popular in the USSR. Besides after-school classes, many of the students enjoy window-shopping, with a stop for a pastry from a café. Some ski or participate in other sports, while others play games.

Every winter brings the Winter Festival, held at the Kremlin Palace of Conferences from December 25 to January 5. Almost everybody going there dresses up in costume. Katya's folk dance class will be one of the performing groups. She and her friends exchange ideas for their costumes. They giggle over the plans some parents have for dressing themselves up.

The most fun is seeing all the adults in costumes. Katya and both her parents plan to spend a whole day at the festival. There will be plays and singers to entertain everyone. Of course, just watching all the silly and inventive costumes is entertainment enough. The Winter Festival is a bright and cheerful holiday during the cold, gloomy days of winter.

Almost everyone dresses up for the Winter Festival.

Katya practices dancing in her costume.

Katya loves to go to these festivals. Besides dressing up and dancing, she can watch the folk dances of other nationalities in the Soviet Union. Sometimes she can even learn some new steps.

It's fun to have time off just to celebrate and be with friends and family. The Soviet government encourages its citizens to work hard because it values labor over all other activities. But everyone needs to relax from their work, so the government sponsors festivals like this, as well as other cultural events and activities.

Katya and her friend, Boria, play with his dog.

When school ends early or Katya has a day off, she hurries to visit her grandfather at his apartment building. If there is still time after her visit, she will see her friend, Boria. He lives in the same building, and they like to play together in the courtyard. Katya and Boria often take his dog out to play.

"You can find him in the snow by his black nose."

The courtyards of apartment buildings make good play areas where children are safe from traffic. Even on very cold days, the courtyards shield the children from the winds. So if school is canceled because of cold, they can often still play outdoors. The white fur of Boria's dog makes him seem to disappear in the snow!

Katya's father is an expert auto welder.

Katya's Family

Katya's father is an expert welder at an auto garage. Katya's mother is a nurse at the same school that her daughter attends. Although her salary is below average, she says, "I get to be near Katya."

Katya's mother, Olya, is from an area in the southeastern USSR known as the Ukraine. Olya grew up in that region and was working as a nurse. She met Sasha when he went there on a business trip. Six months after meeting, they married and she moved to Moscow. Her parents still live in the Ukraine, and Katya's family doesn't get to visit them as often as they would like.

Katya's mother is a school nurse. She enjoys working with children.

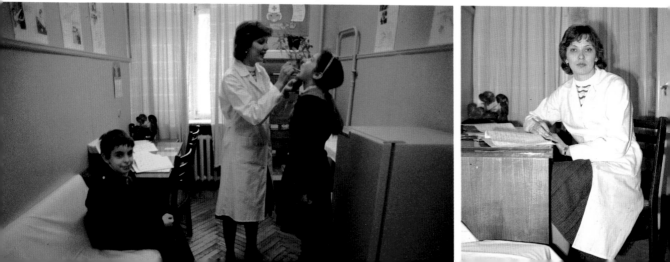

Katya likes to help make the meal.

Pelmeny, a dish like ravioli.

Katya sets the holiday table.

"Company's here!"

Little New Year's

On January 13, Katya's family gathers for Little New Year's. This holiday was once a feast day of the Russian Orthodox church. Until recently, the government closed most places of worship, so families celebrated religious holidays in their homes. Sasha's father, Nikolai, his sister, his brother-in-law, and young nephew celebrate together. Grandfather Nikolai, now retired and living on a pension, was a skilled jeweler who designed and fashioned bracelets, earrings, necklaces, and brooches.

Grandfather's toast: "May the family always be together."

While they eat, Katya entertains everyone with stories of times spent at Grandfather's vacation home near Zagorsk, northeast of Moscow. The backyard opens onto a huge forest, a wonderful place for playing and exploring. Grandfather built the cottage himself and grows vegetables and flowers in his garden.

Grandfather looks forward to Katya's vacations too. "I like teaching her about plants and animals," he smiles.

Katya concentrates on her homework.

Homework

Katya works hard at her schoolwork because she wants to go to a university and study to be a teacher. She knows that only the best students can enter. Right now her grades are very good, all fours and fives. But she knows that if she doesn't keep up, her grades can drop quickly. Sometimes she discusses her homework with friends over the phone. They don't always stick to the subject, but they do try to get some business done before they break into giggles.

Katya also draws. The picture over the desk is one she drew. It is titled "The Earth's Family." Under the glass top of the desk, Katya has arranged pictures and cards she has collected. When homework gets boring or when she needs a rest, she can look over her treasures.

Katya drew her picture after studying the history of World War II. The Russian word for "world" is *meer* and the word for "peace" is also *meer*. So "world peace" is *meeru meer*. This phrase comes up over and over in the Soviet Union and is often proclaimed by posters along the streets. Soviets say, "Peace is the most important thing."

During World War II, the Soviet Union lost over 17 million people, more than any other country fighting in that war. Recently, Soviet troops returned home from a decade-long war in Afghanistan that brought heavy casualties to both sides. So the thoughts of Soviet citizens often turn to world peace. Katya made her poster after listening to her grandfather talk about the cruelty of war. She thought that the world's people should work together like a family for peace.

Two more words are heard everywhere in the Soviet Union today. They are *glasnost*, which means "openness," and *perestroika*, which means "change." The Soviet government wants to improve every area of people's lives. So it is encouraging its citizens to speak out about their concerns. The Soviet government is also revealing facts about past errors and current problems. This seldom happened in the past. Now people are freely exchanging opinions and ideas that may make things better. Already this has brought changes in the nation's economy and political life. Katya is glad to live in this exciting time!

Katya's report card. The grading range is 1-5.

Some of Katya's treasures.

Katya takes over the family desk.

"I might beat you this time!"

Nearly everyone in Moscow, and in many other Soviet cities, lives in apartments. World War II destroyed an immense number of housing units. The Soviet government is building apartment houses to shelter as many people as possible in the quickest way. Because the population keeps growing and many country people are moving into the cities, the need for living space continues to be urgent. So people living in cities will have to crowd into small apartments for some time to come.

Because the apartments in the Soviet Union are small, everyone can't have their own room or even their own desk. Katya's family has a desk they all are supposed to share, but Katya claims it is all hers. She needs room to store her schoolbooks, a place to chat on the phone, and an area to do her homework. So whenever she's home, she'll spend much of that time at "her" desk, working or drawing.

Sometimes, though, she needs a break, so she asks her father to play games with her. Or if the weather is nice, she might want her mother to go for a walk with her. Katya's mother and father are happy to spend time with her. Even though they work during the day, they always find time in the evenings to play or talk together.

When she's not doing homework or playing with her parents, Katya is on the phone. Sometimes she's checking on homework with a friend, but she also just likes to chat. In the winter, it's often too cold to get together outside and visit, so Katya has to rely on the telephone to keep her in touch with her friends.

Textbooks in the Soviet Union aren't much different from those in North America. Katya studies Russian, math, science, history, and literature. She does her homework in small notebooks that the teacher collects.

Katya complains that the family desk top isn't always large enough to hold everything she needs to lay out for an assignment. But somehow she finds a way to do it all and to do it well.

Katya's schoolbooks.   Discussing homework with a friend.

Trolley fare is very cheap.

Subways are clean, fast, and quiet.

Exploring in Moscow

Like most people in Moscow, Katya and her parents ride the trolleys and subways. These are often crowded because not many people own cars.

Cars are expensive in the USSR, and those who can afford to buy one are usually placed on a waiting list. A few people use taxis, but these are costly. Buses, trolleys, and subways run so often and to so many places that they are really the only type of transportation that most people need.

During the Winter Festival, the buses and trolleys are crowded with so many people flocking to the fun. Katya squeezes into a subway car with her parents. At the festival, she puts on her costume and joins her class in dancing a Finnish folk dance. Her parents are wearing costumes, too, like most of the adults. Some of them have on huge funny headpieces. Katya and her parents enjoy the plays and singing of the other groups. Katya says she can hardly wait until next year's Winter Festival.

A Moscow subway station.

Trying out some costumes for the Winter Festival.

On the way to the Winter Festival.

No matter how cold, the trolleys always come along.

A shopper's delight is Moscow's largest department store, GUM.

Katya likes to window-shop along Arbat Street.

When Katya has some free time, she often uses it for exploring Moscow. She especially likes to go window-shopping at GUM, which is pronounced "goom." This is Moscow's largest and most famous department store. The name comes from the Russian initials for words meaning "state universal store." Always crowded, this huge store sells all different kinds of goods.

But Katya's favorite place to window-shop is fashionable Arbat Street, where the shops sell clothes, flowers, antiques, posters, and other items.

Every day, huge numbers of people from small towns come to Moscow for their shopping. Specialty stores are opening up, each selling just one type of goods. Supermarkets are a new development. Katya and her parents often shop in these stores.

Moscow has several lovely parks and outdoor activities that people enjoy even in the winter. One park has a heated swimming pool that stays open all year round. In the parks, children play hockey in the winter and soccer in the summer. In winter, children carrying hockey sticks head for the nearest frozen pond where they play until sunset before going home.

It's time for shoppers to head for home, too, carrying their bags of purchases or just their memories of all the exciting things they have seen and done that day.

Choosing canned foods in a supermarket.

A candy store window is enticing.

Katya's family ends their shopping trip.

Kutuzovsky Avenue, seen from Katya's apartment.

A Visit to Gorky Park

Katya is glad when the snow melts and Moscow becomes green and fragrant with spring. She and her friends happily shed their extra layers of clothes to let the sun shine on their skin as they walk outside. The parks explode with purple, white, red, and yellow flowers.

Summer comes to Gorky Park.

Subway stations are clean and well lighted.

Katya is anxious to get to the park.

Gorky Park is a wonderful place for a summertime stroll.

In May, Katya took exams to pass on to her next grade. Her first exams were in Russian and math. She earned fives in both of them. Now Katya can take more time to relax and enjoy the sun and greenery. During the summer, small boats take people up and down the Moscow River. This is a pleasant way of going from one place to another in the city or just to enjoy the river.

This summer Katya plans to attend Pioneer Camp for four weeks. She wants to learn how to swim. But today she is going with her parents to Gorky Park. They like to spend as many days as possible in the park, enjoying the sun's warmth. By midsummer, it can get as hot as 104°F (40°C). Now that everyone has packed away their thick winter coats, there seems to be more room on the trolleys and subway cars!

There's plenty to see and do in Gorky Park. People can pack a picnic, walk, sunbathe, or play games like soccer or catch. Gorky Park is famous even outside of the Soviet Union. Foreign visitors to the park report on its beauty and its huge size. The park lies in the center of Moscow, almost between the Kremlin and Moscow State University. This makes it convenient for students, business people, and tourists who would like a rest from the day's activities.

Katya likes to run and jump, using energy she has stored all winter. Sometimes her parents can't keep up with her. Katya tells them to hurry up because there is so much to do. Her parents tell her to slow down. But Katya already hears the noise from the amusement park and the disco, so off she runs again.

People line up for their favorite amusement rides.

Gorky Park has woods, an outdoor theater that seats ten thousand people, an amusement park, a disco, and restaurants. Even late at night, there's plenty to do in the park.

The park is a perfect place for a leisurely stroll. It's fun to see how the art students sketch the people around them. And you can always stop to watch the chess players spending hours at this popular game.

Young people like to gather in the disco. Each year there are several rock concerts in Moscow. US or European rock groups tour the Soviet Union once or twice a year. So the young people of Moscow know and enjoy rock music.

Katya loves rock music, too. She likes the band Bravo, but her real favorite is Mashina Vremeni (Time Machine). Some of the Soviet rock bands have become popular in Europe and Asia as well. Katya says, "Russian songs being played in other countries seems like a sign of friendship to me. It's wonderful."

The music of the Gorky Park disco draws Katya to its doors, but her parents have other ideas. The weather is too nice to sit inside and listen to music. So they suggest lunch at an outdoor café, then a visit to the amusement park. Katya gladly agrees.

Lunch outside always seems special.

An enjoyable way to relax.

Katya loves the rides at the amusement park. If she could, she'd be happy every day here, but her family's visit once a month is fine. Her parents go on the rides with her and seem to enjoy all the twists, turns, and swoops. The rides in the amusement park are very popular, so the lines are long. But Katya doesn't mind the waiting. She watches each ride eagerly, then scrambles on for her turn at the thrills.

If the weather is a bit gray or if they need some shade from the sun, Katya and her parents will visit the arcade in the park. There are all kinds of electronic games to play there: pinball, games of skill, target shooting, and competitive games. Katya doesn't always win, but she loves to play. Both parents and children come to the arcade. Here families can have fun together.

Of course, so much activity can make a person hungry and thirsty. So there are plenty of vending machines. Or if Katya is really tired, then they can stop at an outdoor café for a snack and a beverage.

All the fun can't last forever. Soon Katya's parents suggest they head for home. Katya doesn't mind. She knows that soon they'll be back to Gorky Park, her favorite place.

Satisfying a summer thirst.

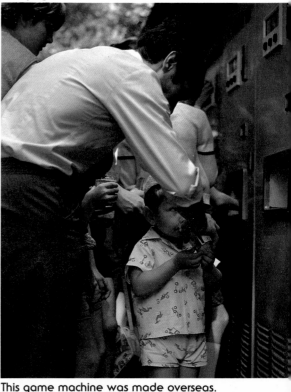

Sasha tries to score a bull's-eye.

This game machine was made overseas.

Pony rides at the Moscow zoo.

A newly wed couple poses in Red Square.

Getting weighed on a city street.

Other Moscow Sights

But the amusement park isn't the only attraction in Moscow. The zoo is a fine place to spend a day. Besides the animals in cages, there are some animals that the children can pet and even ride. Katya is getting too big for the pony rides, but she can watch the animals as they roam their cages or pens. Sometimes they'll perform some surprising antics, especially the monkeys. So Katya greatly enjoys her visits to the zoo.

While they stroll Moscow's streets, they can watch the people who will weigh passersby in the open for a small fee. No one seems to be bothered about their weight becoming known publicly.

One thing Katya loves to see are the newly wed couples in Red Square. The couples go to register their marriage at a government office nearby and then they pose in the square for photographs. Katya enjoys seeing all the beautiful wedding dresses and the lovely flowers.

Katya and other happy campers at Pioneer Camp.

Katya Goes to Camp

For four weeks in the summer, Katya goes away to a Pioneer Camp named Ryabinka. This camp is for the Young Pioneers, the group that she and most of her friends at school belong to. Children learn to play eight different sports here. They also see movies, and three times a week they go to dances.

It's a wonderful way to spend vacation time. Various work places, including Sasha's garage, contributed money to help build the camp. Children between the ages of seven and fourteen can attend. So Katya has a few more summers of camp to look forward to.

Katya is learning to swim.

Katya likes to run.

Working up to a four-meter jump.

Camp lets children try many different sports.

Waiting to enter the dining hall.

Sports raise big appetites!

Games of strategy are popular in the USSR.

There's plenty of good food.

This is a vacation camp, but because the Soviet Union encourages physical labor, work is part of the daily schedule. Near the camp lie the potato fields of the Kolhoz Collective Farm, where the children work and receive wages. They use the money to cover the operating expenses of the camp. Katya pitches in along with the others to get the work done quickly.

After all the sports, work, and nighttime activities, Katya is tired out. Curfew is strictly enforced but even if it weren't, she'd head for bed. Everyone must be ready for "lights out" by 10:00 p.m. At 8:00 a.m. the next morning, the children are glad they had enough time to sleep well. Another active day is always planned.

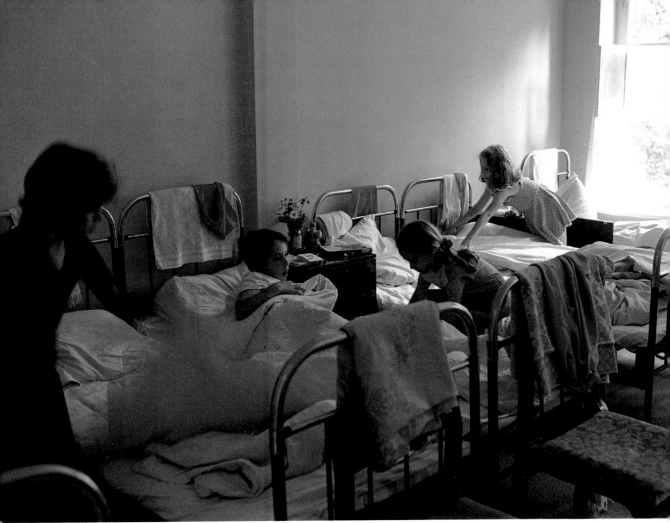

Everyone takes a rest in the middle of the day.

Wash those hands before eating!

Besides all the sports, there are quiet times when Katya can read or play board games and table tennis. The campers rest in the middle of the day, but most of the older ones don't sleep. As summer homework, Katya has to read ten works of literature and write down her impressions of them. For ten days each summer, the fourth-graders help keep the roads and parks clean. Other grade levels do different work.

A huge bonfire marks the end of camp.

This hedgehog lives in the woods nearby.

As the camp draws to a close, the last evening campfire is both a happy and a sad time. The evergreens of the forest surround Katya and her new friends. The children cook snacks over the fire. They sing camp songs and talk about the things they have done that summer and what they plan to do when they go home. Katya looks forward to her family's yearly vacation by the Baltic Sea. This year they will drive there in their own car!

Sasha has bought a Soviet car that cost over 9,000 rubles. This is two and a half times the amount he earns in an entire year, so a car is a real luxury. But he says, "Having a car will give us priceless opportunities for family time, so I don't mind the expense."

A tubful of treats for the campers.

"Come on, sing along. You know the words."

Summer is going by quickly. But for now, Katya will enjoy the warm weather, her friends, the new car, and a few days on the beach. Winter seems very far away as the campers sing cheerful folk tunes, ending with a farewell song.

Time for a last game before saying good-bye.

Moscow at night, one of the world's great cities.

The Historical Museum outside the walls of the Kremlin, center of the Soviet government.

FOR YOUR INFORMATION: USSR

Official Name: Union of Soviet Socialist Republics
(old name: Russia)

Soyuz Sovetskykh Sotsialisticheskikh Respublic
(SOY-yooz so-VYET-skih sohts-ee-ah-lees-TEESH-skesh-keh
rehs-POO-blik)

Capital: Moscow

History

Explorers and Early Settlers

Over 3,000 years ago, nomadic peoples from Asia began migrating over the vast grasslands, known as steppes, north of the Black Sea. The Cimmerians were the first people known to settle there. After them, in the seventh century BC, came the Scythians, to be followed by the Sarmatians, Goths, Huns, and other groups.

Into the forests and meadows north of the steppes came tribes of Slavs from the west in the fifth century AD. They settled as farmers, herders, hunters, and fishermen. Later, they became traders, moving goods from the Baltic to the Black Sea.

48

The Founding of Russia

The Slavs established important trade centers, like Novgorod and Kiev. Because constant tribal feuding kept them from forming a unified state, in 862 the Slavs around Novgorod asked Rurik, a Swedish chief, to be their ruling prince. Since he was a Scandinavian, who were called Rus by the Slavs, Novgorod and the area surrounding it became known as Russia. When Rurik died, a kinsman, Prince Oleg, ruled on behalf of Rurik's young son, Igor. Descendants of Rurik were to be princes and rulers of Russia to the end of the sixteenth century.

Farther south, two other Scandinavians ruled Kiev. To expand his territory, Prince Oleg had them killed and moved the Russian capital to Kiev. He then extended his rule in all directions, reaching as far as Constantinople. Here, in 911, he made a trade treaty with the Byzantine Empire. The Scandinavian Rus rapidly became like the Slavs, learning their language, marrying among them, and adopting their customs. Rurik's descendants conquered other neighboring tribes and expanded the Russian Empire. Kiev, its capital, became an important city.

Vladimir and Christianity

The Russian people worshipped tribal gods. But in 988, Vladimir I converted to Greek Orthodox Christianity. This was the faith centered in Constantinople, the capital of the Byzantine Empire. Vladimir made the new creed the empire's official religion, declared the Russian ruler to be its supreme head, granted the church authority to run most of its own affairs, and ordered its services to be held in the common language of the people. In this way, the new religion became the Russian Orthodox church. Soon after, Byzantine culture greatly influenced Russian architecture, art, and music. Two Christian missionaries, St. Methodius and St. Cyril, brought the Greek alphabet to Russia. With some changes, they used it to teach the Russians how to read and write. It is called the Cyrillic alphabet, after St. Cyril.

The grand duke of Kiev ruled the Russian Empire. But often the man who held this title could not make the princes of the states under him obey his orders. By the eleventh century, these princes continually fought one another in order to enlarge their territory. This made the Russian cities vulnerable to attack from outsiders, particularly the Mongols.

The Mongols were skilled horsemen and fearless soldiers from Asia. Under Genghis Khan, they had conquered much of China and other parts of Asia in the early 1200s. Batu Khan, a grandson of Genghis Khan, led his army, the Golden Horde, to the west, attacking Russia in 1237. After conquering several cities, he destroyed Kiev in 1240. Two years later, Batu established Sarai, his capital, on the lower Volga River near present-day Volgograd. The empire he ruled stretched from Lake Balkhash in Russia to the Danube River in Europe. For over two hundred years, the Mongol rulers collected tribute from the conquered dukes and princes.

The Rise of Moscow

Since the 1100s, Russians had been migrating from Kiev, away from warring princes and raiding nomads. Gradually, other Russian nations developed. Moscow, a military outpost founded in 1147, was ruled by Rurik's descendants. In 1327, Ivan I, the grand duke of Moscow, gained from his Mongol overlord unlimited power over the Russians living in the Moscow area. Ivan also persuaded the Russian Orthodox church to move its headquarters there under his protection.

As Moscow grew in size and importance, its rulers became more powerful. Ivan III, also called Ivan the Great, through war, seizure, and negotiation, gathered many Russian states into one nation under his rule. He made Moscow the nation's capital. By 1480, Ivan the Great refused to pay tribute to the Mongol overlords. By now, the Mongols were divided and warring among themselves, and they retreated without a fight before Ivan's superior army.

When Ivan the Great's grandson, Ivan IV, known as Ivan the Terrible, became ruler in 1547, he declared himself *tsar*, or emperor, of all Russia, becoming the first crowned head of Russia. A ruthless ruler, he greatly extended Russian territory and increased his personal power. Moscow's population grew to about 200 thousand and became an important center of trade.

The Romanovs, 1613-1917

After Ivan the Terrible died, Moscow and Russia were without firm leadership for many years. Finally, a group of nobles and soldiers elected Michael Romanov tsar in 1613. The Romanov line continued to rule the Russian Empire until 1917.

Warfare with Asiatic tribes, Mongol domination, and the self-rule of the Russian Orthodox church kept Russia isolated from European developments for a long time. Then Peter the Great, a Romanov who ruled from 1682 to 1725, decided that his empire should become westernized. Peter made the Russian nobles cut off their long beards, wear shorter coats, and act more like Europeans. He built the first Russian navy, modeled after European navies. He improved the army, and won many battles that extended the area of Russia. He built many schools and universities, factories, and scientific laboratories. He reformed the calendar and established the first Russian-language newspaper. When some Russians argued that they wanted to keep their old Russian ways, Peter often jailed them.

Peter built a new capital for Russia on the Gulf of Finland in order to protect newly conquered territory with a fort and a naval base. Named St. Petersburg, the city became Russia's European seaport. It consisted of palaces, government offices, houses, museums, schools, and shipyards. Peter moved the government there from Moscow in 1712. Many Russian nobles also moved their estates there so they could be near their ruler. St. Petersburg remained the capital for over 200 years.

Catherine the Great was a German princess who later became tsarina of Russia when her husband, the Romanov Peter III, was murdered in 1762. She was much drawn to literature and philosophy, two topics that did not interest Peter the Great. Catherine expanded Russia's boundaries by conquering the neighboring lands of the Crimea and parts of Poland and the Ottoman Empire.

Alexander I, grandson of Catherine the Great, spent most of his reign involved in foreign wars. The French, led by their emperor, Napoleon Bonaparte, invaded in 1812 but retreated when the Russians burned Moscow, an act that deprived his troops of food and shelter. Alexander's pursuit of the French across Europe led to Napoleon's defeat. The Russian officers brought back to their homes the liberal political views of western Europe.

The End of Tsarist Russia

The Russian rulers had occupied themselves with wars that constantly expanded the national boundaries. They were seldom interested in the lot of their subjects. The people continued to live in a feudal society with few rights. Harsh poverty, a restricted economy, secret police, denial of political activity, severe censorship, and widespread illiteracy left the people with no opportunity to improve their lives. When occasionally granted some relief by one tsar, the people soon lost it under the same or another ruler.

When Western political views on the rights of the common man spread among Russian writers, students, the younger nobles, and members of the upper middle class, they realized that Russia was a despotic state. They began forming secret societies to develop ideas for political change.

The work of two political revolutionaries profoundly influenced the revolutionary movements in Russia. Two Germans, Karl Marx and Friedrich Engels, meeting in Paris in 1844, found they shared an identical political outlook. They thought that the workers, rather than the landed and wealthy people, should decide how governments should run. They then collaborated in writing about these ideas and in organizing the international Communist movement. In 1848, Marx published *The Communist Manifesto*, which advocated replacing a society based on wealth, poverty, and class with a society based on working and without any classes. Later, in *Das Kapital*, a three-volume work finished after his death by Engels, Marx urged the people to overthrow capitalists, those people who controlled wealth, and to establish a dictatorship by the workers.

Eventually the various Russian liberal groups, including those of factory workers and peasants, agitated for political and economic reforms. The Russian government reacted by repressing them even more. Near the end of the nineteenth century, many different revolutionary movements began to clash violently with tsarist troops. Strikes and acts of terrorism broke out from time to time. In 1905, uprisings and mutinies brought some slight reforms by the tsar, Nicholas II, who established a parliament but later greatly limited its powers.

The Russian Revolution

In 1914 Russia entered World War I on the side of the Allies, France and Great Britain, who would be joined later by the US, Italy, and Japan. The war severely strained the country's capacity to care for its people, causing shortages of food, clothing, and other supplies for the Russian soldiers and the civilian population. Continued losses on the battlefield made the war unpopular. In 1917, rioting in the capital brought about the abdication of Nicholas II, the last Romanov tsar. The parliament set up a provisional government to manage the country temporarily.

Instead of solving the critical domestic problems, the provisional government decided to concentrate on continuing to fight the war. For several months, there was confusion and lack of clear leadership as various political parties, military groups, and workers' *soviets*, or councils, conflicted with one another over goals. Strikes and demonstrations took place. One party, the Bolsheviks, appealed to workers and expanded into the majority party.

The Bolshevik leader, Vladimir Lenin, had championed Marx's communist views for a long time. To these he now added the idea that Russia should be organized around workers' soviets. In November of 1917, Lenin and Leon Trotsky led the Bolsheviks in the overthrow of the provisional government. The country's name later changed to the Union of Soviet Socialist Republics (USSR). In March 1918, the USSR made peace with its enemies, although the other Allies continued fighting. In the same year, the Bolsheviks executed the former tsar, Nicholas II, and his family. Moscow became the capital of the country, and Lenin became the first head of the USSR. When Lenin died in 1924, the old capital, Petrograd, formerly St. Petersburg, was named Leningrad in Lenin's honor.

After conflicts within the Communist party, Joseph Stalin emerged as the next leader, ruling the Soviet Union from 1929 to his death in 1953. He demanded complete power and he ruthlessly eliminated anyone who opposed his will. In the 1930s, Stalin led an intensive drive to modernize Soviet industry, especially in coal, oil, and iron production. At the same time, he took away most of the freedoms and rights of Soviet citizens. He drove millions of peasants off their land, executing over ten million, in order to establish huge collective farms. The farms are now state-owned, and the peasants work on them for wages, living in nearby villages. Stalin suppressed religion, forbade freedom of speech, and abolished the free press. He established a force of secret police to spy on Soviet citizens. During the infamous purges of the late 1930s, uncounted numbers of people went to prison for political reasons. Within a three-year period alone, three million people died through execution or ill-treatment.

The Soviet Union since World War II

On June 22, 1941, Germany attacked the USSR. For four years the Soviet Union fought the Germans. Over 17 million Soviet people died in World War II. When the war ended, Soviet troops occupied the countries from its western border to the middle of Germany and murdered anyone they saw as a threat. The Soviets established communism in these countries, now called the Eastern European bloc. Included are Bulgaria, Romania, Poland, Hungary, Albania, Czechoslovakia, and East Germany. Because democracy and communism are such opposite systems of government, there was a long period, called the Cold War, during which the USSR and the United States distrusted each other's policies.

The men who ruled the Soviet Union after Stalin faced many serious problems. Under Nikita Khrushchev, housing shortages and crop failures made their citizens discontent. In the 1950s and 1960s, the people in Poland, Czechoslovakia, and Hungary rebelled. The Soviets crushed these rebellions. In 1979, under Leonid Brezhnev, Soviet troops entered Afghanistan to put down the guerrillas fighting the Communists who had taken over the Afghan government. In a war lasting nearly a decade, the Soviets lost 15,000 troops and sustained 35,000 injured before pulling out in 1989 without a decisive victory.

The Soviet Union Today

Today, the USSR faces severe domestic problems. Its industries lag far behind their Western counterparts. Many of the nation's lakes and rivers, like its air, are seriously polluted. And despite its vast farmland, the country must import food every year to feed its people. Mikhail Gorbachev, the present leader of the USSR, seems to be making many positive changes. He has discussed limiting nuclear weapons with the president of the United States, has recalled Soviet troops from Afghanistan, and has declared a policy of *glasnost*, or openness, allowing more freedom of the press and of speech than has been permitted since Stalin's rule.

Government

Governing Bodies

The USSR's 15 states are called republics, but the Communist party controls all the official governing bodies. The people elect the 544-member Supreme Soviet, which is the national legislature. But until 1989, only one candidate ran for each office, an approved Communist party member. The Supreme Soviet meets twice a year. Its job is to approve legislation the party sponsors and to appoint people to offices. One group it appoints is the 39-member Presidium, a council that does the work of the Supreme Soviet when it is not in session. The Supreme Soviet also appoints a president to head the Presidium. Mikhail Gorbachev is currently president.

The Supreme Soviet also appoints a 100-member Council of Ministers, which is responsible to the Presidium but has come to have more power. Like a cabinet in a democracy, the council manages areas such as defense, the economy, mining, and culture. The Supreme Soviet appoints the head of the council, the premier, who today is Nikolay Ryzhkov. Often the president and the premier are the same man, usually the general secretary of the Communist party. The premier is the USSR's most powerful man, except for the general secretary.

Now the Communist party has added another level to its government, a group larger than the Supreme Soviet. Since March 1989, the people have voted for delegates to the newly established Congress of People's Deputies. Some of these candidates are not Communist party members. The deputies, with other deputies elected by official and public groups, will select 544 of their members for a new Supreme Soviet. These groups might represent anything from the Communist party to special interest groups such as the Society of Stamp Collectors.

The Supreme Court is the USSR's highest court, followed by the supreme courts of the republics and the various regional courts. Judges, attorneys, and others in the system are all appointed. Ordinary civil and criminal cases appear before people's courts. Each people's court has a panel of one trained judge and two citizens, called assessors, to assist him in reaching a decision. In most democracies, people go to court over many issues. But in the USSR, civil suits concern only cases of disputed inheritance or of disputed divorces involving children. Attorneys for prosecution and defense work at every court level.

The Communist Party

About 10% of the population belongs to the Communist party. At an all-party gathering, called a Congress, the members elect 400 of their number to the Central Committee. The function of this committee is to approve decisions made by the Politburo, usually done without any discussion. The Central Committee is led by the general secretary, who is currently Mikhail Gorbachev. The Congress also elects the Secretariat, consisting of ten people. The Secretariat, headed by the general secretary, carries out the daily work of running the country. The Central Committee elects the 14 voting members of the Politburo. The Politburo is the most powerful body in the USSR. It meets regularly to decide on matters of national importance. The Politburo selects the general secretary, who presides over it.

Fishing on the Amur River. Sometimes huge catfish are caught here.

Sports and Recreation

Winter sports such as tobogganing, bobsledding, ski jumping, ice skating, and ice hockey are popular in the USSR. In the summer, water sports such as water skiing, yachting, swimming, and scuba diving are popular too. The game most popular in the Soviet Union is chess. Since 1948, all but one of the world chess champions have been from the Soviet Union. Gary Kasparov has been the world chess champion since 1985.

Language

The official language of the Soviet Union is Russian, taught in all Soviet schools. It is written in the Cyrillic alphabet, which resembles the Greek alphabet. Over 300 other languages and dialects are spoken in the Soviet Union, but only about 18 have over a million speakers each. Nearly half the people speak Russian as their native tongue. About a quarter speak other Slavic languages like Ukrainian or Polish. Smaller groups speak Turkic, Armenian, German, Caucasian, Oriental, or other tongues. National tongues are encouraged, but people know they must speak Russian if they want to get ahead.

Land

The land area of the Soviet Union is more than double that of any other country in the world. About the size of North America, the Soviet Union covers about 8,650,000 square miles (22,400,000 sq km). Three-fourths of the land is not suitable for farming and is sparsely populated. The Arctic Ocean borders the USSR on the north, and the Pacific Ocean borders it on the east. The Soviet Union's southern neighbors include North Korea, China, Mongolia, Afghanistan, Turkey, Iran, the Caspian Sea, and the Black Sea. Its western neighbors include the Eastern bloc countries of Romania, Hungary, Czechoslovakia, and Poland. Northwest of the USSR lie the independent nations of Finland and Norway, and the Baltic Sea.

Across the northern part of the country lies the *tundra.* In summer, a few inches of soil melt above the permafrost, a layer of permanently frozen subsoil. Mosses, lichens, and low shrubs grow here. South of the tundra lies a band called the *taiga.* In summer, the soil above the permafrost here thaws deeper than in the tundra. Here grow deciduous and coniferous forests. Large herds of reindeer roam in the forests. South of the taiga rise many mountain ranges, including the Ural and the Caucasus mountains. Farther south stretch the *steppes*, or grasslands, a region of fertile farmland. South of the steppes lie sandy deserts that only a camel can cross. A zone of Mediterranean climate lies around the Black and the Caspian seas, making the region a pleasant vacation area.

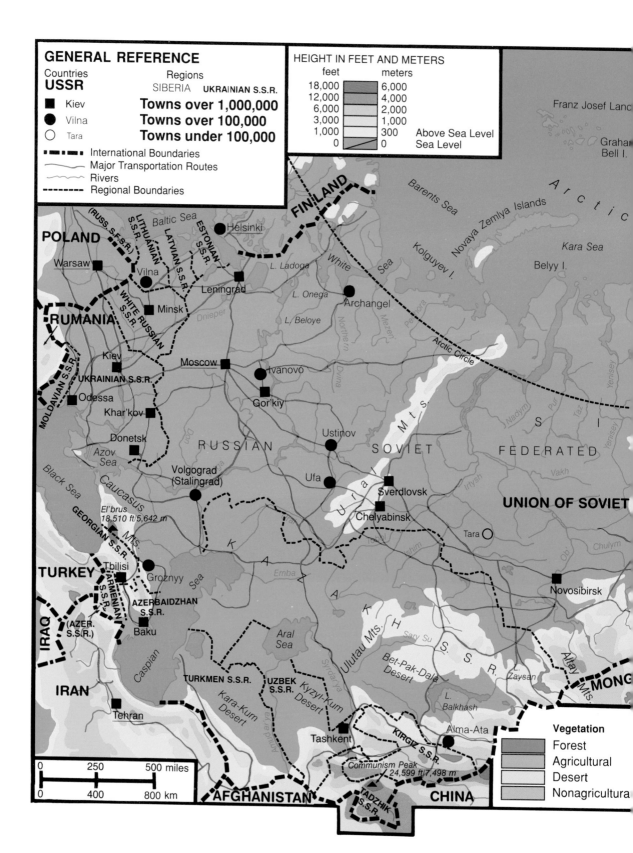

GENERAL REFERENCE

Countries   Regions
USSR   SIBERIA   UKRAINIAN S.S.R.

■ Kiev   **Towns over 1,000,000**
● Vilna   **Towns over 100,000**
○ Tara   **Towns under 100,000**

▪▪▪ International Boundaries
‒‒‒ Major Transportation Routes
~~~ Rivers
‒ ‒ ‒ Regional Boundaries

HEIGHT IN FEET AND METERS
feet   meters
18,000   6,000
12,000   4,000
6,000   2,000
3,000   1,000
1,000   300   Above Sea Level
0   0   Sea Level

Franz Josef Land
Graham
Bell I.

POLAND
Baltic Sea
Helsinki
(RUSS. S.F.S.R.)
LITHUANIAN S.S.R.
LATVIAN S.S.R.
ESTONIAN S.S.R.
Warsaw
Vilna
Leningrad
L. Ladoga
White
Sea
Barents Sea
Novaya Zemlya Islands
Kolguyev I.
Kara Sea
Belyy I.
Arctic

RUMANIA
WHITE RUSSIAN S.S.R.
Minsk
L. Onega
Archangel
L. Beloye

Kiev
Moscow
Ivanovo
Gor'kiy
UKRAINIAN S.S.R.
MOLDAVIAN S.S.R.
Odessa
Khar'kov
Dnieper
Northern Dvina
Mezen'
Pechora
Arctic Circle

Donetsk
Azov Sea
RUSSIAN
Don
Ustinov
Ufa
SOVIET
FEDERATED
Nadym
Pur
Taz
S I
Yenisey

Black Sea
Caucasus Mts.
El'brus
18,510 ft/5,642 m
GEORGIAN S.S.R.
Volgograd
(Stalingrad)
Sverdlovsk
Chelyabinsk
Ural Mts.
UNION OF SOVIET
Irtysh
Vakh

TURKEY
Tbilisi
Groznyy
ARMENIAN S.S.R.
AZERBAIDZHAN S.S.R.
K A Z A K H
Caspian Sea
Emba
Tara
Ishim
Tobol
Ob'
Chulym
Novosibirsk

IRAQ
(AZER. S.S.R.)
Baku
Aral Sea
Syrdarya
Ulutau Mts.
S. S. R.
Sary Su
Bet-Pak-Dala Desert
L. Zaysan
Altay Mts.
MONG

IRAN
Tehran
TURKMEN S.S.R.
Kara-Kum Desert
UZBEK S.S.R.
Kyzyl-Kum Desert
L. Balkhash
Amu Dar'ya

Tashkent
KIRGIZ S.S.R.
Alma-Ata
Communism Peak
24,599 ft/7,498 m
TADZHIK S.S.R.
AFGHANISTAN
CHINA

Vegetation
▨ Forest
▨ Agricultural
▨ Desert
▨ Nonagricultura

0   250   500 miles
0   400   800 km

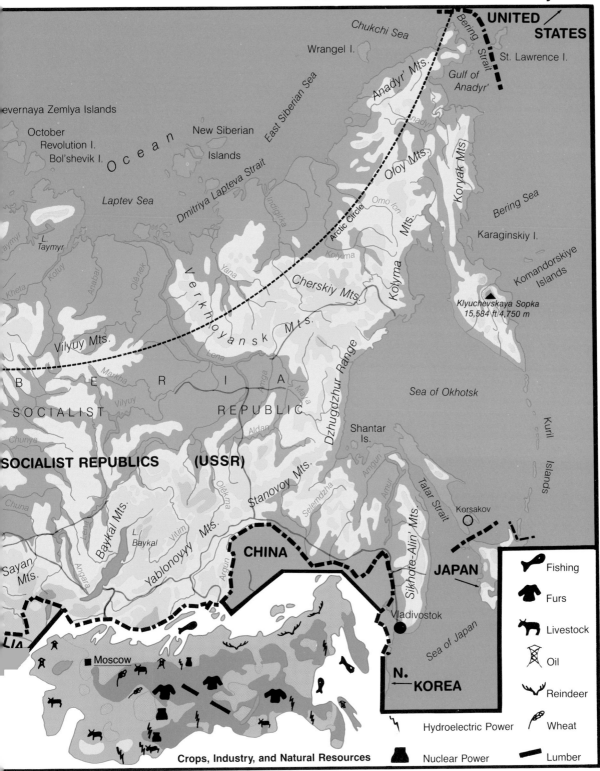

UNITED
STATES

Chukchi Sea

Wrangel I.

St. Lawrence I.

Gulf of
Anadyr'

Anadyr' Mts.

evernaya Zemlya Islands

October
Revolution I.
Bol'shevik I.

New Siberian

Islands

East Siberian Sea

Ofoy Mts.

Koryak Mts.

Bering Sea

O c e a n

Karaginskiy I.

Laptev Sea

Dmitriya Lapteva Strait

Arctic Circle

Omo Ion

Kolyma Mts.

Komandorskiye
Islands

L.
Taymyr

Taymyr

Kotuy

Anabar

Olenek

Yana

Indigirka

Kolyma

Cherskiy Mts.

Klyuchevskaya Sopka
15,584 ft/4,750 m

Kheta

Olenek

V e r k h o y a n s k   M t s.

Vilyuy Mts.

Lena

Markha

Sea of Okhotsk

B   E   R   I   A

Dzhugdzhur Range

Chunya

Vilyuy

Aldan

Maya

Shantar
Is.

SOCIALIST

REPUBLIC

Kuril

Islands

SOCIALIST REPUBLICS

(USSR)

Olëkma

Stanovoy Mts.

Amgun

Korsakov

Chuna

Pit

Angara

Baykal Mts.

Vilim

Yablonoyyy Mts.

Argun

Selemdzha

Amur

Tatar Strait

Silkhote-Alin' Mts.

Sayan
Mts.

L.
Baykal

CHINA

JAPAN

LIA

Vladivostok

Sea of Japan

Moscow

N.
KOREA

Crops, Industry, and Natural Resources

Fishing	
Furs	
Livestock	
Oil	
Reindeer	
Wheat	
Hydroelectric Power	
Nuclear Power	
Lumber	

Climate

Much of the USSR lies near the Arctic Circle, which makes the climate generally cold, although it can vary drastically. The temperatures in the west will average between 5°F (-15°C) and 43°F (6°C) in January. In northeast Siberia, average January temperatures are below -50°F (-46°C). Along the Arctic coast, July temperatures often stay above freezing. Some parts of the Central Asian Desert average above 85°F (29°C) in July. Rainfall also varies widely. Near the Black Sea, up to 100 inches (254 cm) of rain fall per year. Along the far eastern coast, up to 40 inches (102 cm) fall yearly. The average rainfall on the European plain and western Siberia is 16-20 inches (41-51 cm). Central Siberia gets about 20 inches (51 cm) of rain yearly, while parts of the Central Asian Desert average less than 8 inches (20 cm) of rain each year.

Agriculture and Natural Resources

The USSR's most important crops are wheat, potatoes, barley, and sugar beets. They account for over 70% of the total Soviet crop production. Nearly 30% of all cropland produces hay and corn to feed animals. Industrial crops — such as sunflowers and other oilseeds, cotton, flax, and hemp — account for only 3% of Soviet crop production. Cattle, hogs, sheep, and goats are the most important types of livestock. In the far north, herders raise reindeer. Hunters supply hides, furs, and meat. Soviet ships profitably fish in both the Atlantic and Pacific oceans. The country's vast forests of hardwoods and softwoods are harvested for lumber and

Flowering shrubs brighten a Moscow park.

paper products. The USSR has the largest iron ore deposits in the world. Other important minerals are manganese, chromium, copper, lead, zinc, aluminum, platinum, gold, and diamonds. The USSR possesses huge reserves of coal, oil, and natural gas and is one of the world's largest producers of these products. Oil and natural gas supply over 70% of the nation's energy. Most of the Soviet Union's electricity is generated by burning coal, oil, and gas, but the production of hydro-electric power is expanding. Nuclear power plants also add to the production of electricity, and there are plans to build more nuclear power plants.

Industry

Since 1917, the Soviet Union has been expanding its industrial production. The country is best known for its output of iron and steel, and the manufacture of trucks, automobiles, farm equipment, and other heavy machinery. More recently, the Soviet Union has begun to concentrate on consumer products such as washing machines, refrigerators, TVs, and radios. Other industries include clothing, food products, medicines, and chemicals. The USSR is second in the world in industrial production. But personal income levels, living standards, and productivity levels are generally well below those of Western nations. To make industry more efficient, the Soviets are trying methods new to the USSR, such as private cooperatives, self-management for factories, and privately run factories.

Currency

The main unit of money in the Soviet Union is the *ruble*. One ruble equals 100 *kopeks*. Normally, a country's money circulates freely among other nations, and this determines its value. But the Soviet Union does not allow its ruble to circulate freely. Instead, it sets an artificial value on the ruble that does not reflect its real buying power. In 1989, one ruble was valued at $1.60 in United States currency. At the same time, the illegal black-market exchange rate put the value at ten rubles for one United States dollar, which indicates the ruble's real buying power.

Population and Ethnic Groups

In 1989 the population of the Soviet Union was 287 million people, ranking third in population after China and India. There are at least 100 different ethnic groups in the USSR. Three-fourths of all Soviets are Eastern Slavs, including native Russians who make up nearly one-half of the total population. They live mainly near the Black Sea and in the forested regions. People of Turkic descent live in the sparsely settled grassy steppes and in desert oases. People of Caucasian descent, including Armenians and Georgians, live in the southeast. The people of Soviet Estonia, south of Finland, are of Finnish heritage.

Education

Schooling in the Soviet Union is free and compulsory. Children begin school at age seven and attend until they are 17 or 18. They are expected to finish at least the 10th grade, or the 11th grade in non-Russian-speaking areas of the country. But many students in the rural areas leave school earlier. After this schooling, students may attend a night school, a trade school, or a university. About 10% of Soviet students attend the USSR's 900 universities and technical colleges after passing the rigid entrance exams. The government provides tuition, housing, food, and books. Students are encouraged to join the Communist party organization for their age group: the Octoberists at ages 7-10, the Young Pioneers at ages 10-14, and the *Komsomol*, or Young Communist League, at ages 14-28. About 99% of the people are said to be able to read and write.

Religion

The Russian Orthodox church, whose membership is between 40 and 50 million, is the largest religious group in the country. Other major religious groups include Jews, Muslims, Buddhists, Baptists, Lutherans, Roman Catholics, and Armenian Orthodox Christians. The USSR's official religious policy is atheism, which means no belief in any higher power, so the government discourages religious belief. But recently, the government is growing more tolerant of religion. As a result, churches, mosques, and synagogues are reopening, and their congregations are increasing.

Art in Russia and the Soviet Union

Some of the oldest art objects are the religious *icons* that decorated churches and homes in old Russia. An icon is a painting of Jesus, Mary, or a saint on a piece of wood. The colors are bright; red and shiny gold are seen on many icons. The most famous icon is perhaps the Virgin of Vladimir, painted by an unknown artist about 850 years ago. It can be seen in Uspenski Cathedral in Moscow's Kremlin. Many Russian Orthodox churches remind us of old Russia's architecture, built entirely of wood, with wooden pegs used in place of iron nails. Churches, influenced by the Byzantine style, usually bore domes that look like onion bulbs.

In the last 200 years, Russian ballet, established by French masters, has become one of the greatest ballet organizations of all time. One famous Russian dancer was Vaslav Nijinsky, whose sensational leaps amazed everyone. Another famous ballet dancer is Mikhail Baryshnikov, who defected to the West in 1974.

Russia has produced many of the world's great composers. Modest Mussorgsky and Peter Ilich Tchaikovsky are just two who composed music that has delighted the world. Some of Tchaikovsky's most famous works, *Swan Lake* and *Sleeping Beauty,* are often presented by North American dance companies.

Nineteenth-century Russia produced many powerful literary works. Among famous works read to this day are *War and Peace* by Leo Tolstoy, *Crime and Punishment* by Fyodor Dostoyevsky, and the plays and short stories of Anton Chekhov. The work of poet Osip Mandelstam criticized his government, so he was sent to a Siberian labor camp, where he died, probably in 1940. But some modern writers, such as Boris Pasternak and Aleksandr Solzhenitsyn, have now attained recognition in the USSR, as well as worldwide appreciation, for their revealing and critical novels.

A folk dance of Gruzziya in the Caucasus region.

Moscow: The Heart of the Soviet Union

A population of over ten million in the city and the suburbs makes Moscow the largest metropolis in the Soviet Union and the eleventh largest in the world. The city is also the Soviet cultural and economic center. It has many museums, sporting events, exhibitions, and concerts. The most striking place in Moscow is the Kremlin on Red Square. In Russian, *Kreml* means "fortress." The first Kremlin, constructed of wood, was built in 1156 and later rebuilt. The present Kremlin was finished in about 1495. Surrounding it is a red brick wall that extends 1.4 miles (2.2 km). In some places this wall is 65 feet (20 m) high and nearly 20 feet (6 m) thick. The massive wall is a reminder that the Kremlin was originally a fortress. The Kremlin has 20 towers of different heights and designs. The tallest, named for Ivan the Great, is nearly 270 feet (82 m) high. The Kremlin is no longer used as a fortress; it now houses the Soviet government and many fine museums. In Red Square, you can also see St. Basil's Cathedral, with its world-famous onion-bulb domes.

Soviet People in North America

The Soviet government has greatly restricted its citizens' leaving the USSR. Because of this, immigration to North America has been sporadic and in low numbers, except during four periods. First, in 1917, immediately after the Russian Revolution, great numbers of the educated and the aristocracy left. Some settled in the large cities of the United States, but most went to France. Since then, few ethnic Russians leave their country; those who do go to the cities of North America. Immigrants come from every class and age group, and include laborers, skilled workers, and professionals. Among those who migrate are Jews, ethnic Germans, and ethnic Greeks. The first of these people left during the three or four years following World War II. Most were captives released from German concentration camps. Then, in the 1970s, the Soviet government, in return for needed US credits and grain, agreed to permit more of its citizens to leave. And finally, in 1989, the liberal policies of Gorbachev allowed greater numbers of people to leave, even though these migrants included skilled workers needed in the USSR.

Glossary of Useful Russian Terms

da (dah) .... yes
do'braye oo'tra (DOH-bray-eh OO-trah) .... good morning
nyet (nyet) .... no
ostanofka (uh-stuh-NAWF-kuh) .... stop
pazhah'lsta (pah-ZHAH-luh-stuh) .... please
spasee'ba (spah-SYEE-bah) .... thank you
telefo'n (tyee-lyee-FAWN) .... telephone
voda' (vah-DAH) .... water
vy'khat (VIH-khuht) .... exit
zdrah'stvooite (ZDRAHF-stvooy-tyeh) .... hello

More Books About the Soviet Union

Here are some more books about the USSR. If you are interested in them, check your library. They may be useful in doing research for the "Things to Do" projects.

The KGB. Lawson (Wanderer)
Lenin: Founder of the Soviet Union. Resnick (Childrens Press)
Peter the Great: Russian Emperor. Schlesinger, editor (Chelsea House)
Russia: A History to 1917. Resnick (Childrens Press)
The Russian Revolution. Campling (David & Charles)
The Russians in America. Eubank (Lerner)
Soviet Union. Jackson (Fideler/Gateway Press)
The Soviet Union: Land of Many Peoples. Watson (Garrard)
The Soviet Union: The World's Largest Country. Gillies (Dillon)
The Union of Soviet Socialist Republics. Resnick (Childrens Press)

Things to Do — Research Projects

Mikhail Gorbachev's policies of glasnost and perestroika have brought about many changes in the Soviet Union. The research projects below require accurate, up-to-date information from current sources. Two publications that your library may have will tell you about recent newspaper and magazine articles on many topics:

Readers' Guide to Periodical Literature
Children's Magazine Guide

1. In the past, the Soviet government did not permit criticism of many of its former leaders. Now it allows the entire truth to be told. What are the Soviet people finding out about Joseph Stalin, who ruled their country for 24 years?

2. The government of the USSR is now allowing privately owned stores. If you started a restaurant, what kinds of food would be most popular?

More Things to Do — Activities

1. Visit your school or public library and check out a record of Tchaikovsky's music to play at home. Try to find a record of a Soviet rock group to play. Does this music sound different from the music you listen to?

2. If you would like to have a Soviet pen pal, write to these people:

International Pen Friends
P.O. Box 290065
Brooklyn, New York 11229

Worldwide Pen Friends
P.O. Box 39097
Downey, CA 90241

Be sure to tell them what country or area you want your pen pal to be from. Also include your full name, age, and address.

Index